Special thanks to Jessie Chatigny who was my story
wrangler, contributor, and editor.

Cover Design collaboration with Steve Witmer.

www.influxbook.com
www.dannykimm.com
dannykimm@me.com

*To the best transition that's
ever happened to me—EJ*

In Flux
Finding Purpose
in Transition

DANNY KIMM

with Jessie Chatigny

Table of Contents

INTRO-
DUCTION

Introduction

Are we there yet?

That familiar question. Perhaps you remember asking it during a never-ending road trip across the country. Or when you're engaged to your fiancé and the wedding planning days lost their luster. Or maybe you just couldn't wait to have a more fulfilling job, get to the right weight, own a home, or take a year off.

We've all been there haven't we? That proverbial state of uncertainty and unknown, eager for the next steps in life. Our mind, body, and souls enter into a fragile state when we don't know where we are heading.

When you look in the viewfinder of a camera, you only see a small square box. Only one way of perceiving things. When you can step back from the viewfinder, the scope of sight is so much more vast. Away from the lens, context and frame of reference awaits. We need to see transitions from a wider, more dynamic point of view, not from the viewfinder that discomfort often brings.

That's what this book is all about, shifting our perspective when we are in the state of flux. This is a guide to finding purpose in transition.

1: THE STATE OF FLUX

A transition is the space where a passage takes place, where we undergo a change or metamorphosis **that takes us from here to there.**

C hange is inevitable and ubiquitous. We spend our time and resources effecting change, adapting to change, pushing for change, avoiding change, and witnessing change. The Ancients talked about it (panta rhei[1]). Musicians can't write enough about it (ch-ch-ch-changes[2]). We watch characters undergo it on Netflix and track it in friends on Facebook.

While there is a lot to say about change, the flux state in between Points A and B is less addressed yet critically important. Some changes are "effective immediately"—like breaking a leg, losing a job, saying a vow. But for others, that Point B is a bit further off—like rehabbing your leg so you can still make your six-minute mile, finding a new job, becoming a great spouse. With long-arc changes, there is time in between Point A and Point B. Between here and there. That morass of time in between is *in flux*. The state of transition.

A transition is the space where a passage takes place, where we undergo a change or metamorphosis that takes us from here to there. From student to worker. From single to coupled. From child-free to parent. From employed to unemployed. From employee to employer. From dependent to independent to reliant again.

Generally, people don't like hanging out in flux. Most people I interact with in my line of work are uncomfortable with transition, yet simply don't have the tools to navigate it. They ask, "Danny, can you just tell me what I should do next?" It's not that simple. Yet we're there so frequently! As soon as we've achieved one goal, one Point B, we are on to the next, aching to get out of the "here" again. If there was a fast-forward button for transition, it'd be worn out. The author and biochemist Isaac Asimov once said, "Life is pleasant. Death is peaceful. It's the transition that's troublesome."

Why don't we like being in flux? It's uncomfortable. In the "uncertain middle," dissatisfaction with the status quo rises: I can't live like this any longer! Uncertainty and self-doubt grows: *Will I ever get there?* There are real discomforts associated with waiting, even with

LIFE IS PLEASANT.

DEATH IS PEACEFUL.

IT'S THE

TRANSITION

THAT'S TROUBLESOME.

Isaac Asimov

being in transition. You might be living in a house that is too small for your growing family. You might be working in a dead-end job with no prospect of advancing. Or you might have just received your diploma in the mail and you still haven't heard from any prospective employers.

We don't like to be uncomfortable: we loath being in the transition state almost more than the pure Point A state. Why is that? Sometimes we would rather be at Point A because it's predictable and certain, versus the instability of the unknown. We like those "pure" states because there is a perception of control. Expectations and "the rules of the game" seem more clear (e.g. an employee versus a job seeker). Yet, the fear of stepping out of Point A is the root of failing to begin something new. It keeps Point B as a pipe dream instead of inching closer to it.

Flux and Friction

Often when we are in flux, we feel friction. In physics, friction is the resistance that one surface or object encounters when moving over another. Rubbing your palms together makes heat, for example. Friction is uncomfortable because there is resistance. This goes against our natural inclination to "take the path of least resistance." Friction often means that transition is occurring, whether we sense it or not.

But what if our perception of friction in life is incomplete? What if friction, like gravity, is an unavoidable reality in life? And what if, like gravity, you need a little bit? For example, friction in nature is a positive thing. Friction is a sign of movement or momentum. Think about how you get to work every single day. Tires on the vehicle you're riding, whether it's a bus, car, or bicycle, all require friction to move you from home to work and back again. Friction, in just the right amounts, can be a powerful aid in moving through various seasons of life, transitioning us from Point A to Point B. Although we avoid resistance at all costs, being frictionless is **not** the goal. A state of being without friction means no movement, momentum, change, or growth.

Often times when I am coaching someone in transition I will ask them, "What's your friction point?" In other words, what are the things in your life that are causing the most tension, pain, or frustration? They might say, "Well, I'm not happy with my job" or, "I don't have a sense of direction for what to do with my life." Identifying these friction points is key if we want to find purpose in transition. More on that in Chapter 3.

Friction: Just the Right Amount

The good news is, if you are feeling discomfort from a point of friction, this is an invitation. For forward movement to happen, there has to be friction. Too much friction and things catch on fire. Too little, nothing moves and you are simply spinning in place. But that perfect amount, that just right catch, means that change is ready to take place. It means that it's time to get ready for being in flux.

Let's take a look at this graphic (*Figure 1*) to build our understanding of friction and what I call the **Friction Threshold**.

The arc represents the period of transition and the associated rising and falling stress levels. There is the "Inertia Zone", where you are living life in the listless doldrum and where you might feel stuck. No friction means you aren't moving forward. Actually, you might even be moving backwards.

Then take a look at the other extreme. If you

experience friction beyond your personal **Friction Threshold**, you may be at risk for crashing and burning. We'll call this the "Burnout Zone".

Ideally, there is optimal amount of friction in the "Ideal Zone" where friction is the catalyst for momentum and movement.

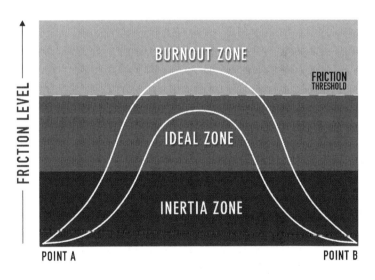

Figure 1: *Friction levels and Friction Threshold*

Questions to consider in the Inertia Zone:

What are my gifts and talents? Am I using them?

. . . .

. . . .

. . . .

. . . .

. . . .

. . . .

. . . .

What emotions do I feel about change? Is the transition the issue or it something else?

. . . .

. . . .

. . . .

. . . .

. . . .

. . . .

. . . .

. . . .

What fears prevent me from pursuing what I'm really passionate about?

....
....
....
....
....
....
....
....
....

What are some things I am unsatisifed with in life? Do I feel stuck?

....
....
....
....
....
....
....
....

Questions to consider in the Burnout Zone:

What are the specific points of friction that I'm experiencing right now?

....

....

....

....

....

....

....

....

What ways will I suspend change in these arenas?

....

....

....

....

....

....

....

List a few things that might be the source of burnout:

+

+

+

+

+

What goals can I create to help pace myself?

....

....

....

....

....

....

....

....

....

....

Questions to consider in the Ideal Zone:

When it comes to change, or living in flux, am I prepared for a sprint or a marathon? How does this feel?

....

....

....

....

....

....

....

What are a few things I am grateful for about change?

....

....

....

....

....

....

....

What rhythms am I creating while living in flux?

. . . .

. . . .

. . . .

. . . .

. . . .

. . . .

. . . .

. . . .

. . . .

Where am I currently in my life and what am I moving towards?

. . . .

. . . .

. . . .

. . . .

. . . .

. . . .

. . . .

. . . .

The more transitions you face, the more friction there will be. Friction is cumulative. For example, when you get a job, it isn't one transition but it might be multiple changes happening at once. A new job might require you to move halfway across the country, take a paycut, meet new co-workers, and require a new schedule. All of those factors increase the the amount of friction during transition. Or maybe you're about to have a baby. Having a baby is one transition. The others that follow are sleep deprivation (at least for the parents), change in friend circles, and an adjustment in scheduling priorities. Transition is not an isolated event, rather a series of events that all build upon each other to increase the level of friction.

As we gain more experience, the more transitions we get under our belt, that **Friction Threshold** rises and we are able to handle more friction with more ease. Do you remember when you had your first job interview? How nervous were you then? Now imagine you have five new companies on your résumé and have had numerous interviews since then. More practice, less friction. Now it doesn't always work perfectly like this but as we journey through life, our experiences increase our capacity and **Friction Threshold**. Friction is a good thing and we have the potential to grow in the changes that come our way.

Frequent and Fertile

I am struck with the irony that we don't have that many words for transition. We have Point A and Point B, but say nothing about the no-man's land between. Hmmm. Is it even important to address the in-flux time? Are transitions worth exploring if we don't even have many words to describe them? Yes, for two reasons: that time in flux is **frequent** and **fertile**.

When you start out in life, it seems like there are only a few transitions, after which it's smooth sailing. You grow up. Get a job. Get married. Start

The time in flux is
FREQUENT
and FERTILE.

a family or business. Boom, done. We emphasize the hereafter, yearning for that state of completion or accomplishment. *Spoiler alert: that never really happens.* While there are certain moments—even sustained times—that are colored with the bliss of achievement, you never really "get there." There are a myriad of changes in life and many happen over time, not instantaneously. That means we each will spend a significant portion of our lives in one transitional stage or another. For every growth, loss, gain, adaptation, there will be a period of transition. **Transition is frequent**.

Growth is often measured by tangible changes: how much did your nephew grow last summer?; when did you decide to change career paths?; did you hear that they got married?; wow, you look really fit! But in my opinion, the measure of growth is not merely the outward appearance; the real growth happens in flux. Although we mark "change" by these outward indicators (e.g. graduation, marriage, weight loss, etc.), discomfort, pressure, transition: those are the periods when we learn more of who we are becoming.

These in-between seasons are filled with lessons for the next chapter in life. For example, I learned a lot about what I wanted or didn't want in a partner right before breaking up with my girlfriend. I learned what kind of job I wanted when I was becoming disillusioned with my first (a period of transitioning out of one career path to another). When we are miserable in flux and beyond our depth, we reach out to mentors, read books, and soak up wisdom. We try things out, experimenting with what works to get any kind of momentum; this often requires friction.

The lessons we learn in hardship stick with us for a lifetime, serving as guideposts for future transitions and in all the Point Bs, if we choose to pay attention and remember them. When working with people who are in that mucky state that is neither here nor there, I try and gently say, "Don't miss the lessons that can only be learned in the in between." There is likely a specific thing that you can only learn in these moments. Maybe patience, resilience, or courage is being built up faster than it could be in a settled, status quo environment. **Transition can be fertile.**

So, humans are in flux in one area or another almost all the time. We almost always do it poorly when there is much to be gained from doing it well. Why aren't we doing it well? Why aren't we even addressing it as a "thing"?

Let's do that, shall we? Let's address our state of flux and get into three tactics that will make transition lighter, smoother, and more fruitful.

Here are the Cliff Notes:

1. Make Space

2. Get Together

3. Love the Pause

Easy enough, right? Well, yes and no. Let's dive in together.

How to use this book

At the end of each chapter, you will have an opportunity to practice living in transition. The first section is called "Transition Praxis". Praxis literally means to practice. The second section is called "Transition Toolbox". Each section is intended to guide your thoughts to pay attention to how you're thinking, feeling, and behaving in states of flux and to apply lessons learned for productive action.

Here's the thing, not every question or praxis will be helpful for you. If it doesn't resonate with you, move on to the next. But remember, don't avoid resistence. I had a mentor tell me once, "Resistence is your friend." What he meant by this was that sometimes resistence is an opportunity to grow. So don't avoid uncomfortable, rather see it as an opportunity to become more of who you already are.

Transition Praxis

1. Describe a time in your life where you were in flux. How did that feel?

....
....
....
....
....
....
....
....
....
....
....
....
....
....
....
....
....

2. *What are some current transitions in your life? Don't worry about fixing it right now. Sometimes, it's just good to name it!*

....
....
....
....
....
....
....
....
....
....
....
....
....
....
....
....
....
....
....

3. How would you describe friction? Where do you see it in your life?

....
....
....
....
....
....
....
....
....
....
....
....
....
....
....
....
....
....
....

4. Not all friction is bad. What was a previous friction point that seemed negative but ended up being positive?

....

....

....

....

....

....

....

....

....

....

....

....

....

....

....

....

....

....

....

....

1: The State of Flux

2: MAKE SPACE

What is your inclination when you feel uncomfortable? **Most of us seek quick comfort.**

Flux. It doesn't feel right. It can feel like hovering above where you should be, or like being stuck in the mud. Neither here nor there. Itchy. *Friction-y*. (New word!)

A few months ago, my wife and I were inspired to get a new dining table. After hours of researching different options, we decided that we could design and craft one just like we had seen online and for less money. We found a local shop where they sell beautiful slabs of wood at all different shapes and sizes. We decided to go with Bay Laurel. All we had to do was fill the holes, sand it, oil it, and put legs on it.

When we first started the project, I was all in. I bought a sander, oil, galvanized piping for the legs. I did the research on how to properly fill the holes with epoxy and stain the wood using oil. But after a few weeks went by, I realized the work wasn't as easy as I had expected. The ramp up was energizing and motivating. But in between the idea and the end result, the energy fizzled out. That piece of wood is still in my backyard, unfinished.

So why does this matter? The middle is the hardest part. Transition can feel this way at times. The freshness of applying for a new job fades, the wonder of being pregnant gives way to weariness, new love hits its first skid. In one way or another, you are probably feeling what most people feel: *stuck.*

What is your inclination when you feel uncomfortable? Most of us seek quick comfort. I go out to dinner with my friends; I go exploring a new neighborhood with my wife. I look at social media, flipping through beautiful snapshots and FOMO-inducing status updates. Maybe you host a party or do some elaborate craft or project. Maybe you daydream about Point B, pinning away. Maybe you go on an endurance run or a Netflix binge. We try and alleviate our unease by masking it, suffocating it, or running from it.

Who wants to marinate in discomfort? Or hang around in a thought space that is full of too many questions and seemingly no answers? I'm going to ask you to do something counterintuitive: bear with me.

What if you sat down and got okay with awkward? Instead of distracting yourself, take time to reflect and see from where that point of discomfort stems. What exactly are you uncomfortable about? Bring it into the light. I firmly believe that when we turn our backs to something scary, something "too big to think about," it grows in our mind's eye. The issue doesn't actually get bigger but it looms behind you, it's shadow licking at the corners of your vision. Face it. Sit with it.

Without making space to understand the transition, we cannot know for certain what the issue in flux actually is. For example, many people think they are uncomfortable in their careers. Some really are, but others end up realizing they are in a relationship that isn't working. Or the stress of trying to have a baby is mistaken for stress with a spouse. Or they think they feel disconnected from their family, but it's really about uncertainty in their own future. They feel the friction, and attribute it to one area of their lives without spending the time to really feel it and think it through.

Making space—consciously setting time aside to spend time thinking—will help you to identify where the friction is coming from. Is it really the job? Or is it your current location, the weather, or that burrito you had last night? Perhaps it's the day-to-day tasks that you're responsible for or the fear of being a father. Ask yourself, "Am I *creating space* to identify the pressures in my life at this current moment?"

Another benefit to making space is to help us discern what our **Friction Threshold** is. Every time we undergo a change or transition, we have the opportunity to learn what our **Friction Threshold** is. How much can I handle given the circumstances in my life right now? Is it different than last time I went through a transition?

I call those issues or particular contentions friction points: think of them as buttons at the center of uncomfortable challenges. When in flux, it's critical to make decisions that fix those exact pain points, not fix something else. It's as if you had a broken arm and are in a ton of pain, but you don't take the time to diagnose the issue. Who knows? You may end up getting a massage when what you needed was an x-ray and a cast.

Every time we experience flux, we have the opportunity to grow our **Friction Threshold**. Our **Friction Threshold** can be similar to physically working out. If you are consistent with it, you have the ability to increase the weight load or the amount of reps in one session. If you add too much weight prematurely, you run the risk of pulling a muscle or burning out too quickly. Awareness that we even have a **Friction Threshold** is a great starting point for transition. Every season of flux is an opportunity to grow.

I also meet with people who don't know they are in transition. Most people can identify discomfort but don't attribute to the season of transition they might be in. Not only do they not know where the pain point is, they don't know they should be looking for one! The only remedy for this is making space to be in flux.

Making room means bringing "the flux" into the light for inspection. Sure, you may not be able to fix the friction point right away, but identification of the problem is the first step in making a plan. With the pain point in sight—the desire to become an entrepreneur, an unmet need in a relationship, purchasing your first home, the drive to get back in shape—you can begin to create a plan for stability and clarity; a road map to Point B.

This is an extremely difficult process. It's challenging to navigate by yourself. Only you know really. You may be running to set up an appointment with a counselor, a coffee date with a mentor, or load up your kindle with books from the experts. Nothing is wrong with any of those things, but I strongly encourage you to spend some time exploring that current friction point by yourself. There is information about your situation and circumstances that only you can fully understand.

When I first got to Cal Poly San Luis Obispo, I thought I was going to become a doctor. My dad is a successful pediatrician and I longed to follow in his footsteps. The status and financial stability of being a doctor were also appealing to me. But as the years went on, I became frustrated with my classes. My classmates all excelled while I fell behind. Then one summer, I was invited to play music with my best friends at a high school summer camp in the mountains of Santa Cruz for two months. Every morning, I would wake up before the sun was out and take a walk in the picturesque mountains. It was during these moments of reflection that I began to identify my friction point. The friction I felt was due to my being on the wrong career path. I realized that I wanted to coach people more than fix them (medically speaking).

Making space is critical. My parents wanted me to become a doctor, my friends and mentors

The flux state isn't a passage of time to be rushed through, rather an opportunity to grow towards who **we are becoming.**

even affirmed this, but deep down inside, I had to listen to the inner voice guiding me to who I was becoming. Without space, that truth would have been drowned out by everyone else's opinion without being attuned to my own passions.

The flux state isn't a passage of time to be rushed through, rather an opportunity to grow towards who we are becoming. Identifying friction points is the beginning of transition. Only when we make space can we begin the process of being okay with where we are even though we aren't sure of what's in front of us or where the path will lead.

How to Make Space

Making space needs to be a conscious choice. It's the kind of thing that will not happen on its own. Sometimes that choice is wrapped up in a murky fear. We are afraid of what knowing the pain point will demand of us. If I know what the problem is, what will this new knowledge require of me? Yes, some of that fear can be merited. It can be arduous to transition out of an old role or into a new stage in a relationship. It may require change and new effort. But take this opportunity to be present with yourself, to pay attention to the lessons that can only be acquired in the state of flux.

I was once coaching a client who was in a precarious state. Even though she had a secure position, her institution was in a serious season of transition with new hires at the executive level. Her direct boss could be modified at any moment and as a result, her role in the organization would have been in jeopardy. As our coaching session began, I could tell that her mind was running a million miles a minute. She was thinking about her tasks and responsibilities, thinking about personnel issues, and mentally juggling the countless meetings ahead of her. As she was processing her schedule, plans, and goals, I stopped her mid-sentence and asked, "How much time are you taking for yourself?"

She looked at me slightly confused and asked, "What do you mean?"

"Well..." I slowly eased in, "I guess I'm asking who or what is taking your time from you?'"

With a puzzled look, she inquired, "Who took my time away? What do you mean by this?"

I said, "It sure sounds like your time is being taken by your tasks, responsibilities, to-do lists and everyone else around you. My challenge for you in this season of organizational flux would be to figure out how to take some of your time back."

All of a sudden, I could see a weight being lifted off her shoulders. She had never been given permission to "*take back her time.*" I then encouraged her to find space every single week and reserve it for herself. Instead of meeting the demands of everyone else, what if she began to allocate minutes to hours of her week to process, reflect, and be present with herself and her needs?

In seasons of uncertainty, these already infrequent moments of "me time" can quickly become squashed by the tyranny of the urgent. Everyone else's demands will be seemingly more important than our own real need for space.

So how do we actually make space if we know it's important in transition? For me, I started a project over a year ago to write 750 words[3] a day. It may seem like a lot, but it only takes 15-20 minutes, depending on how fast you type. I started this because I wanted to capture some of my thoughts and reflect on my emotions. I know you might be thinking to yourself, "But Danny, I'm not an aspiring writer." Trust me, you don't have to be a writer for this exercise to be helpful. Writing can be a therapeutic way to process emotions, feelings, and thoughts. When we intentionally tune into how we are feeling, we can connect both healthy and unhealthy behaviors to our beliefs.

Another way that I've created space in my world is to do an activity that forces me to not think. I know that sounds weird but when we are in a state of flux, there can be a tendency to over think. Recently I started taking yoga classes. One reason is because I have a bad back and my doctor told me I need to stretch more. I hate stretching so I just decided to go to "organized stretching". But, another reason why I chose yoga is because it forced me to disconnect from my iPhone, overcome challenging poses while completely focusing on the task at hand. It was an exercise to be present. Not only was it refreshing for my body but my mind was cleared of the endless circles I found my mind getting lost in.

So it might not be yoga or 750 words, but what are some activities that you can do that might help you clear your mind? Is it surfing? Is it taking a backpacking trip for three days by yourself? Finding space, whatever that looks like will be extremely helpful in flux states. Although the temptation may be to hunker down and work harder and process more, there is incredible value to clearing your mind from the decisions you might have to make in order to step back from the viewfinder that often hinders our perspective.

The Goal of Space

One of my favorite movies is *The Secret Life of Walter Mitty*. The reason why I love this movie is because it is about adventure, courage, and finding one's self. But Walter Mitty's life doesn't start off this way. Walter Mitty (played by Ben Stiller) is a manager in the negative assets sector of Life Magazine and has been working there for sixteen years. Let's just say he has a "frictionless life" and is most likely in the "Inertia Zone"—no movement or momentum. He often fantasizes what his life could look like until he is forced to leave his complacent office with an adventure just around the corner. Mitty is tasked to find Sean O'Connell, an acclaimed yet nomadic photographer, in order to retrieve an essential film strip paramount for the final printed edition of Life Magazine.

Mitty's quest to find O'Connell, however, doesn't come without its challenges. He searches far and wide to find this elusive photographer with the hopes of keeping his job intact when he returns. Just as it seems as though all is loss, Mitty discovers O'Connell poised to take a once-in-a-lifetime shot of a surreptitious snow leopard. When O'Connell finally spots one of thee rare "ghost cats" through his viewfinder, he simply sits back and relinquishes the shot. Mitty is baffled by this gesture.

"When are you going to take it?," Mitty asks O'Connell.

"Sometimes I don't," he replies. "If I like a moment, for me, personally, I don't like to have the distraction of the camera. I just want to stay in it."

"Stay in it?"

"Yeah. Right there. Right here."

The goal of space is clarity. But clarity doesn't always come when we're staring through a viewfinder, metaphorically speaking. Sure, the viewfinder can bring focus and attention to detail,

IF I LIKE A MOMENT, FOR ME, PERSONALLY, I DON'T LIKE TO HAVE THE DISTRACTION OF THE CAMERA. I JUST WANT TO STAY IN IT.

Sean O'Connell

but sometimes it hinders us from seeing the larger, wider perspective. When we create space and are intentional in those margins, a moment of clarity might emerge as a byproduct of our patience. Just like O'Connell, the invitation for space is to be "right there, right here" in the moment, not daydreaming of what life will be like after this season of flux.

Transition Praxis

1. What easy comfort do you turn to in times of uncomfortable flux? Busyness? Social media? Projects around the house?

....

....

....

....

....

....

....

....

....

2. *Think on a current discomfort in your life. Follow the thread as far as you can. What is the source of discomfort? Try to go beyond the symptoms to identify the root of discomfort?*

. . . .

. . . .

. . . .

. . . .

. . . .

. . . .

. . . .

. . . .

. . . .

. . . .

. . . .

. . . .

. . . .

. . . .

. . . .

. . . .

3. How are you creating space to identify the
   friction points in your life at this current
   moment? If you haven't been able to find space,
   what will you do to create intentional space?

. . . .

. . . .

. . . .

. . . .

. . . .

. . . .

. . . .

. . . .

. . . .

. . . .

. . . .

. . . .

. . . .

. . . .

. . . .

. . . .

. . . .

4. In the past, where were you successful in creating space to process? What did that feel like?

....

....

....

....

....

....

....

....

....

....

....

....

....

....

....

....

....

....

Transition Toolbox: How to Identify Your Friction Threshold

After you've given yourself permission to be where you are, make a list of transitions that are in process in your life. Don't worry about fixing the problem, just write them down.

Transition #1:

. . . .

. . . .

. . . .

. . . .

Transition #2:

. . . .

. . . .

. . . .

. . . .

Transition #3:

. . . .

. . . .

. . . .

. . . .

From there, rearrange each transition point in order of highest priority. After that, circle the top two or three that will be the hardest to overcome (or require the most energy). Then, put an asterisk (*) by the ones that are out of your control.

After you finish this part of the exercise, isolate each transition and make a list of items that are byproducts of that major transition. For example, if you're getting a new job the sub-categories might be: a change in salary, new co-workers, new weekly work schedule, a longer commute, etc. Identify all the various friction points that are associated with the larger transition. The more items you list, the higher your friction arc may be and you might be in your personal "Burnout Zone".

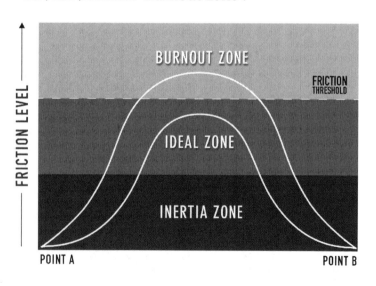

Transition #1:

    Sub-category A

    Sub-category B

    Sub-category C

Transition #2:

    Sub-category A

    Sub-category B

    Sub-category C

Transition #3:

    Sub-category A

    Sub-category B

    Sub-category C

Why do we put an asterisks by the items that we can't control? Simple. Because if we name things we can't control, we free ourselves from trying to control it. For example, your dad may have prostate cancer. You can provide extra support, love, and TLC[4], but you cannot treat the cancer or remove him from the situation. Acknowledge the discomfort that powerlessness brings, but relieve yourself of spinning wheels there—there is no friction to be had.

Making a transition web list like this will help you prioritize each friction point and also help you grow in your awareness of where you stand on the friction arc. The more items there are, the greater the chance for burnout or fatigue. Being in flux is never easy because of the uncertainty of the future, but making a list like this will greatly impact your approach to change. When we are able to diagnose the situation, we have a better chance of making the right adjustments rather than guessing our way down the path.

Transition Toolbox: Creating Space

1. Make a list of things you can do to create space. Don't filter it, just write it!

+

+

+

+

+

+

+

+

2. Circle the top three things that you can do this next week or this month. What are they? Do they take a lot of time?

3. *Now, take a post-it and write one or two things down.*

4. *Stick that post-it note on your desk, your computer, or somewhere where you will see it everyday.*

5. *Your goal is to accomplish these activities in the next 30 days. Go!*

3: GET TOGETHER

[SPACE] AND COMMUNITY BELONG TOGETHER; EACH REQUIRES THE OTHER AS DO THE CENTER AND CIRCUMFERENCE OF A CIRCLE.

Dietrich Bonhoeffer

N ow, are you doing a double take at this chapter's title after the last one? Be alone or get together: which is it? The short answer is both/and.

Dietrich Bonhoeffer, a German Lutheran pastor and theologian, spent his final days in a Nazi concentration camp before he was executed in April 9, 1945.[5] His writings about creating space and belonging in community resonate powerfully with me especially because of his life experiences. Let's see what Bonhoeffer says about this concept:

> [Space] and community belong together; each requires the other as do the center and circumference of a circle. [Space] without community leads us to loneliness and despair, but community without [space] hurls us into a void of words and feelings.[6]

Community and space feed into each other; they are essential to each other. Space is an essential ingredient to knowing yourself. However, knowing yourself (and your friction points) is not enough. Sharing space in community is the next key to finding purpose in transition.

Your Tribe

What do I mean by tribe? I mean a group of people that can share vulnerably and speak truth into each other's lives. A functioning community calls out the best in each of us and challenges us to move ahead in our lives. They give us feedback on where we are so that we aren't left in the dark to make all the decisions ourselves.

Take a moment and think on who is in your corner. If life is like a boxing ring, who is getting you water, bandaging cuts, and whispering advice? Maybe it's a sister, therapist, priest, mentor, or maybe an old friend [**NOTE:** this can't just be someone you hang out with a lot]. These people have to absolutely be rooting for you. *They are your people.*

In times of transition, we are striking out

into unknown territory and your tribe can be the difference between failure and success. Too much space to yourself and you can end up getting lost in your own thoughts. Beyond that, left to ourselves, we might give up altogether with no hope or direction. A tribe's role in these crucial moments help us remember why we are growing in the first place, tenderly encouraging us, and giving us a source of feedback.

In live music, monitors provide the information that tells the musician when he or she is too loud or not in the right place. The sound loop allows the player to receive affirmation or challenge. This is akin to not thinking correctly or taking appropriate action in your life. Feedback can be in the form of your best friend sitting you down and asking some serious questions about a guy you're dating, or a mentor noting your performance in a certain area and suggesting ways to improve. Feedback isn't saying, *Stop playing music!* It's helping the musician figure out how to discover the music they were made to create.

We need feedback especially when in flux. Flux is a time without known markers or timeframes. How do we know how to move forward? Part of moving forward is knowing yourself and building a plan, but a tribe plays a strong role in keeping someone they love on course and heading in the right direction.

This idea of community stands in opposition to both too much space and a network of people that don't support each other. Both reclusiveness and unsupportive communities may have some root in fear: *the fear of being vulnerable.* If I just don't talk about what I'm struggling with, I can get through it and no one will have to know.

A tribe is a place where our greatest weaknesses can be identified yet be affirmed as the place for opportunity and growth. Healthy tribes don't try to fix you, rather, they meet you where you are and help you process the journey you're already on.

I'll never forget the first time I heard a recording of my singing voice played back to me. It was the

Who's in your **corner?**

winter of 2005 and the band I was in decided to record an album. Even though I wasn't the lead singer, I had a few background vocal parts I would contribute to the album. Keep in mind that up until this point I thought I had a decent voice. I thought I could hit backup harmonies with ease. But then I heard my voice, loud and clear through the Sennheiser headphones and I almost immediately took them off. I asked my bandmates, "Is that really how bad my voice sounds?" Sometimes, we aren't as good as we think.

In seasons of flux, especially if you are in the "Inertia Zone," a healthy tribe will have the courage to embolden you to stop eating junk food and get to the gym. Or tell you that, yes, you should buy the ring/apply for the job/take the class. In moments of frustration, they'll be a listening ear for you to vent. In moments of weaknesses, they'll invite you to crash at their place knowing you need a safe haven for the night. In moments of irrationality, they might be just what you need to get you back on the right path.

These kinds of tribes are rare to find. They don't come easy or quickly, but when you find them, they can be the difference between failure and success.

Your tribe can be the difference between **FAILURE** and **SUCCESS**.

The Danger of Destination

One of the reasons why we withhold from sharing the truth of where we are in life is because we subscribe to what I call a **Destination Mentality**. Our culture tells us that the destination is the most important part of being human; getting the dream job, buying a house, getting married with two and a half kids, etc. All of these checkpoints aren't bad things, but when they become the ultimate thing, these checkpoints become finish lines that create unrealistic expectations and feelings of shame if we don't get there. The illusion of reaching these fictitious destinations can often leave us **desperate** or **devastated**.

When the destination becomes the priority, we might become desperate to reach that goal. We cut corners to get a better grade, we network with future employers, not because they are human beings but because they can get you to the next level. We quickly enter into a relationship because the thought of showing up to a party alone leaves us feeling anxious and shame-filled. When we forget that the path between Points A and B is just as important as the final B state, we might choose to act in desperation rather than waiting for things to fall into place.

Another danger of focusing all our energy on a destination is that we might end up feeling **devastated**. The truth is, we might never get "there". Or on the flip side, when we actually reach Point B, we may come to realize that it's not what we thought it would be. Our expectations aren't satisfied. Why? Because our very arrival at Point B transforms it into Point A instantaneously. That means there is another elusive Point B just around the corner.

This **Destination Mentality** can also have a detrimental effect on a tribe. When we feel like we "should have arrived already", we choose not to share our struggles with our tribe for support or advice. Rather than being okay with the in flux status, we hide behind a façade of completeness or wholeness. We are afraid of where we are and we aren't quite ready for the lecture of what we should do to fix our inadequacies. But here's the catch: *we all are always in flux in one way or another*. Let's be honest with ourselves. None of us have arrived. And if you know someone who thinks they have, you may want to share this book with them.

A tribe is often forged through a shared human reality: *incompleteness* and *liminality*. None of

As soon as we give up a **destination mentality** we have the ability to step into reality.

us have arrived professionally, personally, or ideologically. Not even the people who look like they have. Our societies haven't reached her destination either. Just as soon as we reach one milestone, there is another more complex reality to face.

When we recognize and release a **Destination Mentality**, we have the ability to step into reality. This journey called life is a process of who we are becoming—it's okay to be where you are, no matter what people seem to be saying. If we are honest with our truest selves, our shared human experience will allow us to belong. We belong to something bigger than our completion or accomplishments. Our incompleteness is what binds a tribe together.

Your Tribe Takes Time

People in their twenties almost always breathe a sigh of relief when I say this: In your 20s you are figuring out what you're supposed to be doing; in your 30s you are doing what you are supposed to be doing; in your 40s you are perfecting it; in your 50s you are teaching it; and in your 60s you are reinventing. I like the way that this allows for a decade to figure it out. The only caveat is that people can start over midstream—while it might not take a decade to "figure it out" after a switch, it's good to give yourself a little more leeway than you think you'll need. This 20s/30s/40s thing is saying, "Give yourself time for transitions."

With a perspective like that, I think we can both move forward in expecting a supportive tribe and participating in a supportive tribe. When we expect supportive, collaborative communities, we are emboldened to share the vulnerability that is the bedrock of authentic relationships. Without genuine relationships, the feedback loop doesn't work.

But here's the other thing: the way we view our own transitions has a direct impact on how we view our tribe. If we are easily frustrated with our personal state of flux with high expectations and little room for error, we may have this same perspective of what a tribe should be like as well. When we have a short sighted view of ourselves, a **Destination Mentality** might be the filter in how we see a forming tribe. Remember: developing a tribe takes time. So give yourself, and your tribe, space to grow together in the years to come.

Often, when a person is lacking community, no tribe to speak of, the only thing I can advise them to do is start being a tribe. Be a friend. Make the awkward first step at your favorite coffee shop, the office, a MeetUp group, or a place of worship. Connect with a coach or therapist. Offer to help someone move or babysit their kids for an afternoon.

Ride at Your Own Pace

I believe one of the biggest hang-ups preventing true connection with others is the fear of falling behind.

In 2015, I began training for my second California Coast Classic (CCC), a fundraiser for the Arthritis Foundation in which 200+ bicyclists ride down the coast from San Francisco to Los Angeles in eight days. In 2011, I rode my first CCC; I had never owned a road bike before then. The first time around, I meticulously examined the weekly training recommendations and followed them precisely. It was all about making sure I got in the right amount of mileage every week to prepare for something I had never done before. As you can imagine, I was nervous and unsure if I would even survive to tell the tale.

The second time around was a different story. I was way behind on my training schedule. In order to prepare for the eight day ride in September, every Saturday there is a training ride put on by a veteran rider that gets progressively harder as the summer goes on. I jumped in prematurely about half-way through the summer. The first ride I joined said: "30 miles with hills", but I thought to myself, "How hard could it possibly be?". I knew I could ride 30 miles no problem because I had done it before.

As our team took off, I was near the front of the pack. I loved the wind in my hair and at one point I passed one of the elite riders. This rider was older so I psyched myself up: there was no way I was going to be behind this guy. But then we approached our first hill. It was hard; it was long. With each passing cadence, I began to feel my chest get heavy. I could literally feel the muscles in my legs shredding. One by one, the other riders passed me, including the old guy.

Then it got worse. As soon as we got to the top I heard someone shout, "We have two more of those." There was no way I was going to make it. I was already near the back of the pack and we were only on the 12th mile. Thirty miles didn't seem so short after all. Funny, my legs weren't the thing that bothered me the most. It was the fact that the other riders were kicking my butt. A few years ago I secretly enjoyed hills because I was able to race to the top and pass several people along the way. But this year's training had been quite the opposite; I was the last one up.

The sad part is that sometimes we feel like this in life, don't we? We train, we work hard, but it always seems like we're behind somebody else, including people in our tribe. As I minced gingerly around my office the next day, I made note of some of the lessons I'd learned on the ride that I think applies to living in flux and sharing in community.

1. **Fear of Falling Behind.** The truth is, we all have to ride at our own pace. There is no point in riding faster than you've trained for. There's no point in beating yourself up for not going as fast as the rider next to you. The only way to truly be in community is to be okay with who you are, both your strengths and weaknesses.

2. **Fear of Not Measuring Up.** Don't let comparison get the best of you. Rather, let your tribe propel you. Even if you get passed

by people "you-think-you-should-be-faster-than", it's way better to ride together than alone. When we let pride get in the way joining in, we lose the opportunity of a shared experience. Working together while in flux to achieve your goals will foster an authentic tribe.

3. **Fear of Beginning.** Don't let others' success keep you from starting. I've been trying to unlearn the lie that if I am not successful then I shouldn't even begin to try. When we look at other people's Point Bs, sometimes we can give up even before we give it a shot. The lie says, "If someone is better than you, you

RIDE AT YOUR OWN PACE.

might as well give up before you even start." I've found that the best motivation has been surrounding myself with people I aspire to be like who are further along than I am. Don't let their success hinder you from reaching your own. Use it as motivation.

Don't give up. You may be closer to the crest than you think. Just keep pedaling with your tribe.

Belonging

Being in transition can either be exhilarating or incredibly stretching. The truth is, we are constantly in a state of flux to various degrees, it's unavoidable.

One time I was with my tribe and we went around to share how our weeks were. Mind you, this group is made up of young professionals in a extremely transient season of life. As each person shared, I was startled by the overwhelming reality that everyone was in a state of flux. Everyone was moving from one degree to another. Some were dissatisfied with their careers and were hunting for a new job but didn't know where to start. Others had just broken up with a significant other and were grieving this loss. Some were dissatisfied with their spirituality and were on a quest to change the status quo. We were all in transition—none of us were immune to it.

As we shared our struggles and pending uncertainties, I found myself asking the question: "Why don't we share about our transitions more often?" And to take the question even further: "Why don't we share the baggage that comes with being in flux?" I think somewhere in our lives we were told—explicitly or implicitly—that the in-between state is not good, that it is something to keep to yourself. Often times the praise we receive from accomplishment or completion overshadows the lessons learned in the process; every failure leading to success. The destination is glorified often at the expense of slow and gradual growth.

That night our group realized that when we share our flux states, we are creating a tribe of vulnerability. A tribe that is okay with the incomplete and messy reality of life. The inability to give a "correct" or "right" answer is sobering but when we come to a place where we are okay with flux, we have the opportunity to connect with people who have either crossed that bridge or are currently crossing it with you. When we share the friction points, true community is birthed. A tribe that values process over completeness. A tribe that is more concerned about authentic growth than impressed by a diploma that hangs over one's desk.

Vulnerability vs. Transparency

If we want to thrive in our tribes, we have to take this concept to another level. Have you ever thought about the difference between vulnerability and transparency? For most people, transparency is quite easy. We share our "feelings", we share our experiences, we share what we saw in that moment and that's that. Most of the tribe's I've been apart of are good at transparency. But vulnerability goes deeper than that. It invites the listener to participate in the healing process that we are currently in. Vulnerability allows others to be invited into the most secret parts of our stories, uncertain of what will happen to them. Listen to what C.S. Lewis has to say about vulnerability:

> To love at all is to be vulnerable. Love anything and your heart will be wrung and possibly

broken. If you want to make sure of keeping it intact you must give it to no one, not even an animal. Wrap it carefully round with hobbies and little luxuries; avoid all entanglements. Lock it up safe in the casket or coffin of your selfishness. But in that casket, safe, dark, motionless, airless, it will change. It will not be broken; it will become unbreakable, impenetrable, irredeemable. To love is to be vulnerable.[7]

Insert "fear of falling behind" here. Insert "fear of the in-between" here. Fear hinders our ability to be vulnerable with each other—the fear of rejection, the fear of failure, the fear of loneliness are byproducts of a **destination mentality**. And yet a true tribe doesn't mind an incomplete status. A tribe fully present in the process is necessary for anyone going through transition.

So what would your life look like if you had a tribe that wasn't just transparent but vulnerable? What would our communities look like with this radical perspective? And what would our world look like if we all become a little more vulnerable?

Transition Praxis

1. Who is currently in your tribe? How did you find them and what drew you to them?

....

....

....

....

....

....

....

....

....

....

....

....

....

....

....

....

....

2. What is an example of authentic community that has made an impact in your life?

....

....

....

....

....

....

....

....

....

....

....

....

....

....

....

....

....

....

3. What are some ways you could participate in (or build up) a tribe this month?

. . . .

. . . .

. . . .

. . . .

. . . .

. . . .

. . . .

. . . .

. . . .

. . . .

. . . .

. . . .

. . . .

. . . .

. . . .

. . . .

. . . .

. . . .

. . . .

. . . .

4. How might you go about building community for the long-haul?

. . . .

. . . .

. . . .

. . . .

. . . .

. . . .

. . . .

. . . .

. . . .

. . . .

. . . .

. . . .

. . . .

. . . .

. . . .

. . . .

. . . .

. . . .

. . . .

. . . .

5. What keeps you from engaging in your tribe, honestly and vulnerably?

. . . .

. . . .

. . . .

. . . .

. . . .

. . . .

. . . .

. . . .

. . . .

. . . .

. . . .

. . . .

. . . .

. . . .

. . . .

. . . .

. . . .

. . . .

Transition Toolbox: Forming a Tribe

The best place to start with forming a tribe is to be the kind of tribe member you would want to surround yourself with. Write down all the qualities you would want in a tribe member.

Ideal Qualities for Your Tribe:

+

+

+

If you only have two or three things, I know you can think of more.

+

+

+

+

Then ask yourself this question: "Do I personally embody these characteristics? If not, why not?"

....
....
....
....
....
....

From there, make a list of people who you would consider to be part of your tribe. If you don't have anyone, think of people who you think would challenge and motivate you. These people aren't just your friends! They are people who will say the hard stuff because they are more concerned with your growth than making you feel good in that moment.

Ideal People You Want in Your Tribe:

+

+

+

Reflect on why you chose these people. What qualities do they have?

. . . .

. . . .

. . . .

. . . .

. . . .

. . . .

. . . .

. . . .

. . . .

. . . .

The next step is the hardest. Give each person a call this week just simply to catch up; no strings attached, no agenda. Then call them the following week, same thing.

After two or three conversations, either via phone or in-person, share about the current state you are in. From your reflections from your "making space," share with your tribe what you are personally going through. From there, if you feel comfortable, ask them, "Do you feel like there is anything in your life that is "in flux?" When they speak, listen, don't fix. Be present. This simple act of sharing incompleteness is the spark to an authentic tribe.

4: LOVE THE SILENCE

Somewhere we know that without **SILENCE** words lose their meaning, that without listening speaking no longer heals, that without distance closeness cannot cure.

Henri Nouwen

One of my favorite features on the iPhone is the timelapse function. Watching the clouds move in real time, change is almost imperceptible. But with timelapse, you can set up your camera on a rock, sit back for the next few hours, then come back and condense the footage into high-speed. Hours become seconds: clouds race across the sky, a flower opens with the morning. And apparently I'm not the only who loves timelapse videos—they are some of the most popular things out there on social media. We can't help but watch them.

So, what's our obsession with timelapses? They alter time in such a way that it becomes bitesize and accessible. We can see it all there and that feeling gives us a sense of control. Humans love trying to manipulate time. It's why we invest into stocks, buy Crockpot, watch replays (or DVR our favorites), love planning for the future, and have endless hard drive space for photos to record the past.

Controlling time makes us feel better. We like being able to move quickly through the "bad" and hold tight only to the "good." Well, where does that leave transitions? For most, we would fast forward through them if we could, getting out of flux as soon as possible.

The Music of Silence

Music has always been part of my life. I started violin lessons at the age of six. By the time I was nine, I was enrolled in two orchestras and traveled around town to participate in various recitals. Music is in my blood: my mom was a pianist and organist for our church. My dad was the choir conductor and taught me how to play guitar.

In the spring of 2016, my wife and I traveled to the Czech Republic, Austria, and Germany. On our bucket list was to see a classical concert while we were in Austria. One evening, we sat in a lush concert hall in the Salzburg castle overlooking the Alps. In this moment my love for classical music was resurrected from my adolescent years. I quickly found myself transported to another time period as I recalled some of the more famous pieces that I had played growing up as a child; the intricacies of each measure, each movement, each pause.

In that concert hall I was drawn into a memory. One day, when I was about twelve, our conductor stopped our youth orchestra in the middle of our three hour rehearsal and said, "Some of you are rushing the rests!" *How do you rush the rests?* I thought to myself. Rests are, well, silence. Nothing. No notes. How can you possibly rush nothingness?

After a little bit of rehearsal, we figured out that my entire section was counting too fast, rushing through silence in order to play the right notes. But if you play a right note at the wrong time, it's the wrong note!

Silence is a note in music but also a note in life. Silence is essential for transition. It can be a vulnerable space, it can be lonely. Are we meant to feel empty and alone as often as we are in transition? I don't think so. I think we can learn to love the pause that transitions bring. Think of the silence—that space in between the cloud movements, the music, and Points A and B—as transitional space. Silence is necessary and so are transitions.

Remember, that transitions are going to happen

Silence is a **note in music** but also an **a note** in life.

a lot. A. Lot. Small ones weekly, big ones more often than not, many from corners of your life where you weren't expecting transition. If you can break out of the "timelapse" approach to transition and allow yourself to match the rhythms and tempos that are part of life, you'll have a deeper appreciation and more endurance for the pace required to succeeding in flux.

Then, let's recognize the gifts that flux brings. Specifically, rest and learning.

Resting in Flux

Now, the rest that transition brings doesn't feel restful unless you allow it to be so. I think of this couple that I provided premarital counseling once. For a little background: they were young and came from a religious background that places a high value on marriage. Half-way through our second session, they jokingly said, "We think it might be easier to just go to Vegas and elope," because the wedding planning days had lost their luster. They were ready to hustle out of a period of transition: a prolonged engagement was an obstacle that hindered them from moving on to the next chapter of life. I nervously laughed and said, "I remember when I once thought about that…" and then quickly moved on to the next section of the premarital packet.

What I didn't say (and should have) is that this period of waiting can be framed as a period of rest, an invitation to love the pause. A time to do be restored, gather your strength, and be present with your tribe for the unknown challenges that Point B will bring. In this case, becoming an excellent spouse and partner in life.

Being engaged is an especially good analogy. You've found the right person; you can't wait to start the adventure together! You're a team so let's get this party started already. Marriage can be infinitely more challenging and more rewarding than we can imagine. That transition time—between being single and being committed—is best used in preparation. It's the perfect time to learn more intimately about each other. You can ask questions that you didn't ask in the beginning of a relationship, but should be addressed before marriage. (Should we have children? How many? How much student loan debt do you have? Which side of the family will we visit during the holidays?) This way, the flux is used as a time of preparation to order one's life in hopes of a better, more real connection with one another.

To reconnect with the metaphor of music, remember that rest notes are an essential part of music. If you're a musician and have ever played along with a novice musician, there is very little space in their craft. They play, play, and over play in order to compensate for their lack of understanding of rest—they don't confidently relax in the uncomfortable silence in between each note and phrase. But a seasoned musician, now that's a different story. They pause, listen, reimagine, then enter again with grace. They know their moment to play will arrive and are comfortable in their genius not to wear themselves out by rushing to the next note. Music is only complete with rest notes that are *played.* In the same way, the more comfortable we can be with *radio silence*, the more present we will be with ourselves and the flux states in between.

Another example is, when you look at flux as *rest* instead of *limbo*, you can see time between jobs as restorative. Well, at least a little bit. While the very real financial pressures will persist, you just might be able to see the silver lining of being able to go to the beach on a Monday in August, or develop a new hobby you've always dreamed of or travel to a foreign country for a month. Come the fall, when you have a new job, that rest on the beach will help fuel your work day at your new office. Don't miss what rest can offer.

This rest is a foil to the activity of life, helping us manage and appreciate the different phases of life. The silence in between helps us reflect on our limits and transitions us from one movement to the next.

Learning in Flux

A favorite author of mine, Jeff Goins, says in his book *The In-Between: Embracing the Tension Between Now and the Next Big Thing*:

> [...] as we embrace the wait, we learn to appreciate the delays and postponements that teach us some things in life are worth waiting for [...] A life filled with movement, with constant motion and no rest stops, isn't a life at all. It's tourism.[8]

The most important benefit to being in flux, the real reason you should learn to love the pause, is that it is such a productive time of learning. There are lessons in life that can only be learned in the experience of first-hand discomfort and transition.

Listen to this amazing story about Chester Greenwood of Farmington, Maine. In the winter of 1873, Greenwood invented the earmuff at the age of 15.[9] How did he do this? He came up with this idea while ice skating during the frigid winters in Maine. One day he asked his grandmother to sew tufts of fur between loops of wire to cover his cold ears. Now, I guarantee that if Greenwood didn't have frosty ears he would have never invented the earmuffs. The discomfort of skating with chilled ears was the impetus for starting an earmuff revolution! He was a culture shifter because when he first stepped on the ice rink with tufts of fur covering his ears, all his

A LIFE FILLED WITH MOVEMENT, WITH CONSTANT MOTION AND NO REST STOPS ISN'T A LIFE AT ALL. **IT'S TOURISM.**

Jeff Goins

friends made fun of him. Now, not only are these earmuffs functionally useful, in some contexts, they are a fashion statement! These in-between, uncomfortable moments can sometimes be the catalyst for creativity and innovation.

Do you have to learn in transition? No. It's possible to miss a vital period of growth. You might change externally but remain the same internally. In *Transitions: Making Sense of Life's Changes*, William Bridges writes:

> [...]change is situational. Transition, on the other hand, is psychological. It is not those events, but rather the *inner reorientation and self-redefinition* that you have to go through in order to incorporate any of those changes into your life. Without a transition, a change is just a rearrangement of the furniture. Unless transition happens, the change won't work, because it doesn't 'take'.[10] (Emphasis added.)

This flux state is the laboratory in which we learn the most about who we really are. What does this particular transition say about you? How will it help deconstruct who you are stripped away of the day-to-day movements of your life? Because one day, you may need to teach these invaluable life lessons to someone else; a mentee, a son or daughter, a grandchild, and if you miss these moments, you may miss the opportunity to pass these experiences along. Don't miss the moment.

Transition Praxis

1. What does "silence" (metaphorically speaking) look like in your life?

....

....

....

....

....

....

....

....

....

....

....

....

....

....

....

....

....

....

2. *How can you practice restoration into your own time of transition?*

. . . .

. . . .

. . . .

. . . .

. . . .

. . . .

. . . .

. . . .

. . . .

. . . .

. . . .

. . . .

. . . .

. . . .

. . . .

. . . .

. . . .

. . . .

. . . .

. . . .

3. Describe any instinctual resistance to embracing silence as a key in transition.

....
....
....
....
....
....
....
....
....
....
....
....
....
....
....
....
....
....
....

4. *How might consciously choosing to be okay with silence shape they way you approach the next season of life?*

. . . .

. . . .

. . . .

. . . .

. . . .

. . . .

. . . .

. . . .

. . . .

. . . .

. . . .

. . . .

. . . .

. . . .

. . . .

. . . .

. . . .

. . . .

5. What are you learning about yourself in this transition?

....

....

....

....

....

....

....

....

....

....

....

....

....

....

....

....

....

....

....

Transition Toolbox: Love the Pause

Reflect on this past year. What transitions did you face?

....

....

....

....

....

....

....

What Point Bs did you come to and what was the process like?

....

....

....

....

....

....

....

....

Does the flux seem clearer now that you can reflect on it?

....

....

....

....

....

....

....

....

I want you to try something this month. Every Friday, I want you to take 15 minutes and journal what the week was like. Was it frantic with very little space between your day-to-day activities? How much time did you spend with loved ones, or with people in your tribe? As you reflect on your week, ask yourself, "Do I want my next week to look like this?"

If the answer is no, then spend the next 10 minutes making a list of three things that you will do to pause and enjoy the silence. That could be taking a walk during your lunch break. It could be pausing on that project for your house in order to rest. Maybe it's leaving work early so that you can spend time with your child. It might sound scary, but maybe you need to spend a few days away from your significant other in order to make space for yourself.

3 things you will do to enjoy the silence:

+

+

+

During these intentional "getaways," reflect on how your body responds to the space you created. Did you like the space? Where did your mind wander to? How did your emotions respond to the silence?

....

....

....

....

....

....

After you identify your state, ask yourself these deeper questions: Am I feeling any emotions right now? (If not, you are likely in a state of inertia: ask yourself if you want to be there.) What is the root of these feelings? Are they negative? What do these feelings say about the expectations you place on yourself? Are they healthy or unhealthy expectations?

....

....

....

....

....

....

....

....

....

....

....

....

....

....

Now, write down any new insights you gain from these moments of silence. Don't force it. Just be present with it. Is there something you want to leave behind or take with you in the coming weeks?

....

....

....

....

....

....

....

....

....

....

....

....

....

....

....

....

....

As you build momentum for this exercise, try to build this habit into your day-to-day routine. These moments of reflection and self-awareness are critical in our development and growth.

5: RESIL-
IENCE

RESILIENCE IS ALL ABOUT BEING ABLE TO OVERCOME THE UNEXPECTED. SUSTAINABILITY IS ABOUT SURVIVAL. THE GOAL OF RESILIENCE IS TO THRIVE.

Jamais Cascio

Author and futurist Jamais Cascio says it this way, "Resilience is all about being able to overcome the unexpected. Sustainability is about survival. The goal of resilience is to thrive."

Some transitions have the ability to paralyze us with fear. Sometimes that change is dramatic and forced, like in this next story. Whether dramatic or minor, there is a key to surviving any transition and thriving on the other side: resilience.

Thirty years ago, two friends set out to climb Mt. Washington in New Hampshire. Conditions weren't perfect but these two experienced climbers thrived in competition—man vs. wild. As the day progressed, the light snowfall advanced into blizzard-like conditions. The visibility went from minimal to abysmal and they were forced to find any shelter they could find. The friends spent the next few days and nights in their makeshift cave.

Embracing each other for warmth and comfort, they knew most likely they wouldn't make it. Hope was buried and the disintegration of mind and body was unrelenting. Just as they thought that all was lost, they saw a silhouette approach in the dawn's light. They were airlifted to a hospital.

One of the men, Hugh Herr, would have to have his legs amputated; a reality that he, an experienced climber, never had imaged for himself. Herr's transition was not easy; it was devastating to say the least. For most people, having the very thing you love most in the world stripped away from you would be the end of the rope, the end of the story, hope dashed. But for Herr, his resilience was the light to see this accident as an opportunity. Listen to what Herr had to say on the Ted Stage:

> I didn't view my body as broken. I reasoned that a human being can never be "broken." Technology is broken. Technology is inadequate. This simple but powerful idea was a call to arms, to advance technology for the elimination of my own disability, and ultimately, the disability of others. I began by developing specialized limbs that allowed me to return to the vertical world of rock

and ice climbing. I quickly realized that the artificial part of my body is malleable; able to take on any form, any function—a blank slate for which to create, perhaps, structures that could extend beyond biological capability.[11]

Herr went back to school in mechanical engineering biophysics and currently serves as an associate professor in MIT's Program in Media Arts and Sciences. His emphasis is on developing wearable robotic systems that serve people who are in similar situations and his experience is the motivation for innovation. These augmented human appendages are advancing technology in ways never before imagined.

Resilience is finding the grit to make the most of the cards we've been dealt. It's about using what has happened as guideposts and inspiration for the future, no matter the circumstances. Winston Churchill says it best: "Success is the ability to go from failure to failure with no loss of encouragement." The reality is we will fail, and fail a lot. Our expectations for what our paths should look like won't always match reality, but the question remains: who are you becoming through these ever persistent states of flux?

SUCCESS IS THE ABILITY TO GO FROM FAILURE TO FAILURE WITH NO LOSS OF ENCOURAGEMENT.

Winston Churchill

In The Geography of Genius by Eric Weiner, he recounts his quest to figure out what the key ingredients are for making a genius, more specifically if there is a perfect situation or location for where geniuses are born. Here's a brief summary of where geniuses are born:

> One of the biggest misperceptions about places of genius, I'm discovering, is that they are akin to paradise. They are not. Paradise is antithetical to genius. Paradise makes no demands, and creative genius takes root through meeting demands in new and imaginative ways. Creativity is a response to our environment. The problem with paradise is that it is perfect and therefore requires no response.[12]

This is good news for those in uncomfortable flux. Creativity is never born in the ease of paradise; neither is resilience. Resilience is a response to struggles, trials, and unforeseen circumstances—this is both the beauty and blight of life.

PARADISE

CRUSHES

CREATIVITY.

Why This Matters

In the times between here and there, we will experience some of the most challenging obstacles we have to face. But our perspective will determine whether we see obstacles as liabilities or new opportunities. And if we are able to hold on to resilience, our perspective is more closely aligned with seeing the states of flux as the birth of a new chapter.

A few years ago, Joey had a successful finance

job at a large company and was making more than he could ask for as a young man. He was determined to accumulate wealth believing that money would make him happy. But after tireless work weeks and a lack of purpose in his job, he quickly became discontent with his rat-race lifestyle. He decided to quit his job and travel the world for a year with his savings, living more or less as a nomad.

When his bank account dwindled, he returned and entered into a stark, harsh transition. He was trying to get back up to speed, adjust to the pace of life at a now-unfamiliar home, and see how his year off had shaped his career options.

When I talked with Joey about this adventurous season of life, he looked at me with a confused stare. He said, "Honestly Danny, I feel like I wasted my time and now I'm behind on my career. I don't know where to start."

His look said it all: the discomfiture of flux had sent him reeling into questioning his decisions and how it was beginning to affect his present circumstances. "Danny, it seems like the past year was a waste and I feel stuck in where I'm at in life."

I said, "Joey, I don't think that year was a waste. How you look at your year of travel is just as important as why you traveled in the first place.

Maybe there was something invaluable you learned that I bet if you spent a little time creating space in your life to reflect, you might rediscover it."

We were able to talk through ways his travel experiences could help him be a better candidate for jobs he was pursing. Rather than viewing his year abroad as a waste, we mapped out the different ways he grew and how he could apply this newfound experience to the season he was in and where he was heading.

Joey needed resilience to carry on through the difficulties of transition. Resilience is the lynchpin between past experiences, present circumstances, and the hope for what is to come. When we look at every transition as an opportunity to grow, we can develop our friction capacity and ultimately cultivate our resilience. Life is not simply about the beginnings, it's also about finding the courage to begin again.

Resilience is discovering the **SILVER LINING** in our worst transitions.

Transition Toolbox: Growing Your Resilience

As a science major, my goal was never to make assumptions in the lab but to always start by making a hypothesis, then testing and observing. The state of flux hardly feels pleasant enough for reflection and observation. But one of the best ways to gain perspective on a transition state is to take a minute and cool your thoughts. Pretending to be your own life's scientist can give you the emotional room you need to 1) see the opportunities in transition, 2) calm any fears of change, and 3) choose your next steps.

#1 Hypothesis

Treating your understanding of your transition as a hypothesis and not a forgone conclusion is key to staying curious in flux. Being curious is key to reaping in the lessons that can be had in this fragile state. A hypothesis is an educated guess to the reasons for your situation but doesn't assume answers or simply brush the transition under the rug. My suggestion is to think of a few hypotheses that might be viable for your transition.

Life is not simply about the beginnings, it's also about finding the courage to begin again.

These are the guidelines for creating your hypothesis: first, lay out the "issue." Let's say you recently broke up with a long term partner. Or, you aren't sure of your major. Outline it as simply as possible. The second part is create a few underlying reasons for the transition. Sometimes the reason is obvious, but more often than not, these reasons remain a mystery. Let's look take a look at a few hypotheses for these examples.

Example A:

That relationship didn't work out because I was not ready for a serious commitment and I have other priorities.

Or,

Perhaps the relationship didn't work out because I have a lot of work to do on my own before making something work with someone else.

Example B:

> I am super unhappy right now. I think it's my job: I'm in the wrong industry.

> Or,

> I feel deeply discontent. I've lost touch with what I actually enjoy.

Example C:

> Even though I chose math as my major because I was good at it in high school, maybe this isn't the best match for my skill set or where I want to be.

> Or,

> I don't feel as "natural" in my major as I thought I would. I think that this is just the nerves of adjusting to college life as a whole.

#2 Testing

Testing is about being curious about the transition itself and exploring potential answers outside the initial answer we assume. Like I said, it can be difficult to be an observer when you are caught up in the situation. I like to pretend the circumstance in a vacuum-sealed room and I am making observations on the other side of the window.

Testing for Example B above, regarding job friction and transition, could be:

1. Take a personality profiling inventory, like Myers Briggs, Enneagram, or StrengthsFinder and evaluate your day-to-day responsibilities to how you are actually wired.
2. Connect with a career coach or mentor to process your discomfort.
3. Schedule informational interviews with peers or professionals in other fields of interest.
4. Create a plan to research other industries and options.

#3 Observation

Mindful observation helps assess the truth (or lack of) in your hypothesis in order to gain greater clarity on your situation. I suggest asking questions of yourself that are geared to support healthy observations:

1. What do see from your transition? Keep looking for another minute (or more) than you initially want to. Make a list of new things you notice and questions you have.
2. What do you wonder about what you see? How could you find answers?
3. Were the results on track with your hypothesis?
4. Any surprises?
5. Journal any "take-aways" to apply to the next transition time.

#4 Reflection / Inspiration

What happens when you can't change the situation? Or the learning moments are simply out of your control? What if it seems impossible to learn something new? Reflection is where you can be honest and present with your feelings. Not every transition is "changeable" so to speak. It's okay if you feel stuck and the previous steps don't seem to hold up.

The two key factors for this last element are **permission** and **inspiration**. You have to be okay with the flux you're in, even if it's just temporary. Give yourself **permission** to feel your all your emotions—the good, the bad, the ugly. When your expectations don't meet reality, you have the right to be disappointed.

But don't let negative reflection get the best of you. Choose **inspiration**. This exercise is designed to uncover glimpses of inspiration that will last a lifetime. Inspiration looks at every situation as an opportunity to grow, not a waste. But inspiration doesn't stop there. Inspiration is about others. When we are inspired by our resilience moments, we can come alongside others who are currently going through similar seasons of life. Don't give up right away, rather, realize that these all-too-frequent transitions are vital moments that are shaping us into who we are becoming and giving us touch points to empathize with others.

Transition Praxis

Let's try it. Think of a difficult situation that is currently in your life and write it down.

My transition is:

. . . .

. . . .

. . . .

. . . .

. . . .

. . . .

Hypothesis

Try to think of three different explanations describing why you are in this situation and reasons for it?

Hypothesis 1

. . . .

. . . .

. . . .

. . . .

Hypothesis 2

. . . .

. . . .

. . . .

Hypothesis 3

. . . .

. . . .

. . . .

Test

What will you do to test these hypotheses?

Test 1

. . . .

. . . .

. . . .

Test 2

. . . .

. . . .

. . . .

Test 3

....

....

....

Observation

1. What do you wonder about what you are
uncovering? How could you find answers?

....

....

....

....

....

....

....

....

....

....

....

....

....

2. Which hypothesis seems to be most reasonable from after your tests? Were the results on track with your hypothesis?

. . . .

. . . .

. . . .

. . . .

. . . .

. . . .

. . . .

. . . .

. . . .

. . . .

. . . .

. . . .

. . . .

. . . .

. . . .

. . . .

. . . .

. . . .

. . . .

3. What "aha" moments did you have? What is
   something that surprised you?

. . . .

. . . .

. . . .

. . . .

. . . .

. . . .

. . . .

. . . .

4. What lessons did you learn that you want
   to apply to the next time you're in a similar
   transition?

. . . .

. . . .

. . . .

. . . .

. . . .

. . . .

. . . .

. . . .

Reflection

Feelings are real. What feelings do you resonate during this transition? Is it sadness, grief, frustration, excitement or anxiety? Circle your dominant emotions below:

Happiness	Surprise	Trust
Contentment	Anticipation	Fear
Anger	Awe	Loyalty
Sadness	Disapproval	Grief
Joy	Distraction	Remorse
Serenity	Worry	Dissatisfaction

On the next page, in the left column, imagine yourself before this transition began (before you started school, had a newborn, a new job, etc.). What expectations did you have about your transition? How did you think you would feel? What was the desired outcome? What did you think this transition would lead to?

Then, on the right side, write down all the ways this transition or process has or hasn't met reality. What are the the actual results of your transition? Where are you currently in your transition?

Expectations

Realities

Did your expectations meet the reality you are in? Describe the gap between the the desired outcome and the realities you are currently in.

....

....

....

....

....

....

....

....

....

....

....

....

....

....

....

....

....

Now, choose *inspiration*. Write down three things to grow from this experience.

What I've learned...

....
....
....
....
....
....
....
....

Who I'm becoming....

....
....
....
....
....
....
....
....

What I want to give away...

Remember: inspiration means using our experiences to help others. How might this situation help you empathize with others in the future?

....
....
....
....
....
....
....
....

CON-
CLUSION

THE WORD PATIENCE MEANS THE WILLINGNESS TO STAY WHERE WE ARE AND LIVE THE SITUATION OUT TO THE FULL IN THE BELIEF THAT SOMETHING HIDDEN THERE WILL MANIFEST ITSELF TO US.

Henri Nouwen

As I write this book, I am currently in a season of pause. After years of being in vocational ministry, I believe it's time for me to step out in a different direction and pursue a new career path. Everything that I've built my résumé for is in a state of disorientation. My career was being built to be a church planter and lead pastor in the future. Now, I'm in the middle of making a big shift, muddling through what this will look like for me and my family.

How do I feel? It's challenging. It's hard. I am hopeful, but I don't have a guarantee answer or Point B. I don't know which chess piece will move next. I don't have any contract for a new gig waiting in the wings—I don't even know exactly what my working life will look like in the next five months. Yet, I know enough about transitions to make space to identify friction points, take time to learn about myself and take in what this moment has for me.

I'm asking myself the same question I've asked of clients countless times: "What is the lesson I might miss if I'm not able to live in this current state of flux?"

I'm also thinking a lot more about what Henri Nouwen said:

> The word patience means the willingness to stay where we are and live the situation out to the full in the belief that something hidden there will manifest itself to us.

Everyone has to wait. But patience isn't in just the waiting: it's waiting in willingness, in expectancy and hope. There is a difference between waiting and patience. Waiting is passive. Patience, on the other hand, is building character while one is waiting. I'm challenging myself not to miss this moment and committed to curiosity: how will my character be forged during this time?

These three elements—*making space*, *getting together*, and learning to *love the pause*—will make the frequent, all-too-common in-flux times more fruitful and more comfortable.

NOT IN HIS GOALS

BUT IN HIS

TRANSITIONS

MAN IS GREAT.

Ralph Waldo Emerson

. . . .

Transitions. Living in flux. Not only are we on the hook for doing transitions our whole life through, I believe that we were built for doing transitions. We are made to live in the uncertain middle and constant state of change. We weren't made just to merely survive in flux, we were made to thrive in it. We are most human when we are invited to learn, to connect with others more meaningfully, and to face our truest selves in the midst of all of life's uncertain transitions.

In Flux

Conclusion

References

Chapter 1

1. Panta Rhei means everything flows in ancient Greek. http://www.training.co.il/index.php/en/panta-rhei-%E2%80%93-the-story-behind-the-name.

2. "Changes" is a song by David Bowie, originally released on the album Hunky Dory in December 1971 and as a single in January 1972. https://en.wikipedia.org/wiki/Changes_(David_Bowie_song).

Chapter 2

3. 750words.com

4. TLC means "Tender Loving Care".

Chapter 3

5. Dietrich Bonhoeffer. https://en.wikipedia.org/wiki/Dietrich_Bonhoeffer.

6. Bonhoeffer, Dietrich. "Life Together." HarperOne 2009.

7. Lewis, C.S. "Four Loves." Mariner Books 1971.

Chapter 4

8. Goins, Jeff. "The In-Between: Embracing the Tension Between Now and the Next Big Thing." Moody Publishers 2013.

9. Chester Greenwood. https://en.wikipedia.org/wiki/Chester_Greenwood.

10. Bridges, William. "Transitions: Making Sense of Life's Changes." Da Capo Press 2004.

Chapter 5

11. Ted Talk. https://www.ted.com/talks/hugh_
    herr_the_new_bionics_that_let_us_run_climb_
    and_dance?language=en

12. Weiner, Eric. "The Geography of Genius."
    Simon & Schuster 2016.

Acknowledgments

First, I want to thank my Lord Jesus Christ for giving me the ability to write, speak, and love people. "For in him I live and move and have my being" (Acts 17:28).

I want to thank my wife, EJ Kim, who never gives up on me and constantly reminds me to silence the negative voices in my head. Thank you for believing in me and challenging me to share this book with the world. I couldn't have done it without you.

Finally, I want to thank my mentor, friend, and colleague Michael Dauphinee who has been a catalyst for all my professional endeavors and has shown me what it means to live and lead courageously.

About the Author

Born and raised in Los Angeles, CA, Danny Kimm is a growing storyteller and inspiration catalyst. His passion to communicate through words, music, and video are his gift to the world. His dynamic style and personality helps him challenge people to be the best version of themselves.

As a catalyst, Danny creates space for inspiration, motivation, and lasting change for individuals and organizations. His experience, knowledge, and unique abilities in personality assessments and coaching methodologies have given him the platform to develop paradigm shifts in people's personal and professional lives.

Danny is a classically trained violinist, world explorer, and a Laker fanatic.

Booking

If you are interested in booking Danny for speaking, workshop facilitation, career coaching or writing , please inquire at:

DannyKimm@me.com

Or visit

dannykimm.com

In Flux

References